Friendship is a gift from God
that's blessed in every part...
born through love and loyalty...
conceived within the heart.

January 1

You can never change the past. But by the grace of God, you can win the future. So remember those things which will help you forward, but forget those things which will only hold you back.

RICHARD C. WOODSOME

December **31**

Rejoice with those who rejoice;
mourn with those who mourn.

ROMANS 12:15

January **2**

When a friend calls to me from the road
And slows his horse to a meaning walk,
I don't stand still and look around
On all the hills I haven't hoed.

ROBERT FROST

December **30**

A living, loving God can and does
make His presence felt, can and does
speak to us in the silence of our hearts,
can and does warm and caress
us till we no longer doubt that
He is near, that He is here.

BRENNAN MANNING

January **3**

Perfume and incense bring joy to the heart,
and the pleasantness of one's friend springs
from his earnest counsel.

PROVERBS 27:9

December **29**

Our road will be smooth and untroubled
no matter what care life may send;
If we travel the pathway together,
and walk side by side with a friend.

HENRY VAN DYKE

January 4

There is an exquisite melody in every heart. If we listen closely, we can hear each other's song. A friend knows the song in your heart and responds with beautiful harmony.

December 28

To have a friend is to have one of the sweetest gifts that life can bring; to be a friend is to have a solemn and tender education of soul from day to day.

AMY ROBERTSON BROWN

January 5

The life I touch for good or ill will
touch another life, and that in
turn another, until who knows where
the trembling stops or in what far
place my touch will be felt.

FREDERICK BUECHNER

December 27

Let the morning bring me word
of Your unfailing love,
for I have put my trust in You.
Show me the way I should go,
for to You I lift up my soul.

PSALM 143:8

January 6

Many merry Christmases, many
happy New Years. Unbroken friendships,
great accumulations of cheerful
recollections and affections on earth,
and heaven for us all.

CHARLES DICKENS

December **26**

We are all travelers in what John Bunyan calls the wilderness of this world, and the best that we find in our travels is an honest friend. He is a fortunate voyager who finds many. We travel indeed to find them. They are the end and the reward of life. They keep us worthy of ourselves; and when we are alone, we are only nearer to the absent.

ROBERT LOUIS STEVENSON

January 7

The angel said to them, "Do not be afraid. I bring you good news of great joy that will be for all the people. Today in the town of David a Savior has been born to you; He is Christ the Lord."

LUKE 2:10-11

December **25**

A true friend is one who is concerned about what we are becoming, who sees beyond the present relationship, and who cares deeply about us as a whole person.

GLORIA GAITHER

January **8**

God grant you the light in Christmas,
which is faith; the warmth
of Christmas, which is love...the all
of Christmas, which is Christ.

WILDA ENGLISH

December 24

Lord, who hast taught to us on earth
This lesson from above,
That all our works are nothing worth,
Unless they spring from love;
Send down thy Spirit from on high,
And pour in all our hearts
That precious gift of charity,
Which peace and joy imparts.

CHARLES WESLEY

January 9

God became a man. While the creatures of earth walked unaware, Divinity arrived. Heaven opened herself and placed her most precious one in a human womb.

MAX LUCADO

December **23**

As water reflects a face,
so a man's heart reflects the man.

PROVERBS 27:19

January **10**

But you, Bethlehem…
out of you will come a ruler
who will be the shepherd
of My people Israel.

MATTHEW 2:6

December **22**

Some of the most rewarding and beautiful moments of a friendship happen in the unforeseen open spaces between planned activities. It is important that you allow these spaces to exist.

CHRISTINE LEEFELDT

January **11**

When God's Son took on flesh,
He truly and bodily took on, out of pure
grace, our being, our nature, ourselves....
Now we are in Him.... We belong
to Him because we are in Him.

DIETRICH BONHOEFFER

December **21**

When one door of happiness closes,
another opens; but often we look so long
at the closed door that we do not see the
one which has been opened for us.

HELEN KELLER

January **12**

You are a true friend
Pointing me to Him
Lifting my downcast eyes
Turning my wandering gaze to the sky
Proving your love again
You are a true friend.

TWILA PARIS

December **20**

Many women...have buoyed me up in times of weariness and stress. Each friend was important.... Their words have seasoned my life. Influence, just like salt shaken out, is hard to see, but its flavor is hard to miss.

PAM FARREL

January **13**

To receive a gift, molded from love
and sacrifice, selected with care
and tied up with all the excitement
the giver has to offer, is indeed rare.
They don't come along often,
but when they do, cherish them.

ERMA BOMBECK

December 19

A word aptly spoken
is like apples of gold in settings of silver.

PROVERBS 25:11

January **14**

In true friendship…I give myself to my friend more than I draw her to me. I not only like doing her good better than having her do me good, but also would rather have her do good to herself than to me.

MICHEL DE MONTAIGNE

December **18**

His thoughts were slow,
His words were few,
and never formed to glisten,
But he was a joy to all his friends—
You should have heard him listen.

WAYNE MACKEY

January **15**

How does one keep from "growing old inside"? Surely only in community. The only way to make friends with time is to stay friends with people.

ROBERT MCAFEE BROWN

December **17**

I especially value the friends
who love me as God loves me—
through no merit of my own!

SHARON M. MASON

January 16

"**F**or I know the plans I have for you,"
declares the Lord, "plans to prosper
you and not to harm you, plans
to give you hope and a future."

JEREMIAH 29:11

December **16**

Friendship is unnecessary, like philosophy,
like art. It has no survival value; rather
it is one of those things that give value
to survival.

C. S. LEWIS

January **17**

Happiness is being at peace, being with loved ones, being comfortable. But most of all, it's having those loved ones.

JOHNNY CASH

December 15

Yet this I call to mind
and therefore I have hope:
Because of the Lord's great love
we are not consumed,
for His compassions never fail.

LAMENTATIONS 3:21-23

January **18**

For somehow, not only at Christmas,
but all the long year through,
the joy that you give to others
is the joy that comes back to you.

JOHN GREENLEAF WHITTIER

December 14

A friend is one who incessantly pays us the compliment of expecting from us all the virtues, and who can appreciate them in us.

HENRY DAVID THOREAU

January 19

All the things in this world are gifts
and signs of God's love to us. The whole
world is a love letter from God.

PETER KREEFT

December 13

Indeed, we do not really live unless we have friends surrounding us like a firm wall against the winds of the world.

CHARLES HANSON TOWNE

January 20

The Lord has made proclamation
to the ends of the earth:
"Say to the Daughter of Zion,
'See, your Savior comes!
See, His reward is with Him,
and His recompense accompanies Him.'"
They will be called the Holy People,
the Redeemed of the Lord.

ISAIAH 62:11-12

December 12

Our business is to love what
God would have us do. He wills
our vocation as it is: let us love that,
and not trifle away our time in
hankering after other people's vocation.

FRANCIS DE SALES

January **21**

At the end of your life you will never regret not having passed one more test, not winning one more verdict, or not closing one more deal. You will regret time not spent with a husband, a friend, a child, or a parent.

BARBARA BUSH

December 11

I no longer call you servants, because
a servant does not know his master's
business. Instead, I have called you friends,
for everything that I learned from
My Father I have made known to you.

JOHN 15:15

January 22

Dare to love and to be a real friend.
The love you give and receive is a reality
that will lead you closer and closer
to God as well as to those whom
God has given you to love.

HENRI NOUWEN

December **10**

A friend is one to whom one may pour out all the contents of one's heart, chaff and grain together, knowing that the gentlest of hands will take and sift it, keep what is worth keeping, and with a breath of kindness, blow the rest away.

DINAH MARIA MULLOCK CRAIK

January 23

In time, if we walk long enough with Jesus as our friend, He will reveal Himself in newer, deeper, and sometimes even fearful ways. "Don't be afraid," He whispers. "It is I." If we don't have to be afraid of God, we don't have to be afraid of anything.

MICHAEL CARD

December 9

Friendship is not diminished by distance or time...by suffering or silence. It is in these things that it roots most deeply. It is from these things that it flowers.

January **24**

The scripture was fulfilled that says, "Abraham believed God, and it was credited to him as righteousness," and he was called God's friend.

JAMES 2:23

December 8

Attention to detail is the secret of success in every sphere of life, and little kindnesses, little acts of considerateness, little appreciations, little confidences...they are all that are needed to keep the friendship sweet.

HUGH BLACK

January **25**

Too often the I-can-handle-it-myself society we live in seems to promote loneliness rather than friendship. Friends are an important part of sharing the burden and worry of each day.

SHERI CURRY

December 7

Now to Him who is able to do immeasurably more than all we ask or imagine, according to His power that is at work within us, to Him be glory in the church and in Christ Jesus throughout all generations, for ever and ever!

EPHESIANS 3:20-21

January 26

Act kindly, for the hands are fair
That lift another up,
A cup of water you can bear
E'en in a little cup.

VICTORIAN CHILDREN'S VERSE

December **6**

There is something very powerful about...
someone believing in you, someone giving
you another chance.

SHEILA WALSH

January **27**

It is my calling to treat every human being with grace and dignity, to treat every person, whether encountered in a palace or a gas station, as a life made in the image of God.

SHEILA WALSH

December 5

Thank You, God in heaven, for friends.
When morning wakes, when daytime ends,
I have the consciousness of loving
hands that touch my own,
of tender glance and gentle tone.

MARGARET SANGSTER

January **28**

If you are offering your gift at the altar and there remember that your brother has something against you, leave your gift there in front of the altar. First go and be reconciled to your brother; then come and offer your gift.

MATTHEW 5:23-24

December 4

Sweet is the memory of distant friends!
Like the mellow rays of the departing sun,
It falls tenderly, yet sadly, on the heart.

WASHINGTON IRVING

January **29**

True prayer is simply a quiet, sincere, genuine conversation with God. It is a two-way dialogue between friends.

W. PHILLIP KELLER

December 3

Praise be to the God and Father
of our Lord Jesus Christ, the Father of
compassion and the God of all comfort,
who comforts us in all our troubles,
so that we can comfort those in any
trouble with the comfort we ourselves
have received from God.

2 CORINTHIANS 1:3-4

January **30**

We don't accomplish anything in this world alone...and whatever happens is the result of the whole tapestry of one's life and all the weavings of individual threads from one to another that creates something.

SANDRA DAY O'CONNOR

December 2

We cannot tell the precise moment when friendship is formed. As in filling a vessel drop by drop, there is at last a drop which makes it run over; so in a series of kindnesses there is at last one which makes the heart run over.

SAMUEL JOHNSON

January **31**

My friend is not of some other
race or family of people, but flesh
of my flesh, bone of my bone.
This person is my real brother or sister.

HENRY DAVID THOREAU

December **1**

Friendship is like love at its best: not blind but sympathetically all-seeing; a support which does not wait for understanding; an act of faith which does not need, but always has, reason.

LOUIS UNTERMEYER

February **1**

Do not be anxious about anything,
but in everything, by prayer and petition,
with thanksgiving, present your requests
to God. And the peace of God,
which transcends all understanding,
will guard your hearts and your
minds in Christ Jesus.

PHILIPPIANS 4:6-7

November 30

There is danger that we lose sight of
what our friend is absolutely, while
considering what she is to us alone.

HENRY DAVID THOREAU

February **2**

True friends are distinguished
in the crisis of hazard and necessity;
when the gallantry of their aid may
show the worth of their souls and the
loyalty of their hearts.

ENNIUS

November 29

The Lord will guide you always;
He will satisfy your needs in a
sun-scorched land
and will strengthen your frame.
You will be like a well-watered garden,
like a spring whose waters never fail.

ISAIAH 58:11

February **3**

I would maintain that thanks are the highest form of thought, and that gratitude is happiness doubled by wonder.

G. K. CHESTERTON

November 28

A true friend inspires you to believe the best in yourself, to keep pursuing your deepest dreams. Most wonderful of all, she celebrates all your successes as if they were her own!

February 4

I found the sun for me this morning.
I thank You, Lord. I found the warm water
in the shower. I praise You. I found the
bread in my kitchen this morning, Lord.
I thank You. I found the fresh air as
I stood out the door. I praise You. For all
that I see that You do for me,
I thank You. For all that I do not see
that You do for me, I praise You.

CHRISTOPHER DE VINCK

November 27

Happiness is as a butterfly which,
when pursued, is always beyond our
grasp, but which, if you will sit down
quietly, may alight upon you.

February 5

How great is the love the Father has lavished on us, that we should be called children of God! And that is what we are.

1 JOHN 3:1

November 26

Can we find a friend so faithful,
Who will all our sorrows share?
Jesus knows our every weakness:
Take it to the Lord in prayer.

JOSEPH SCRIVEN

February **6**

To be grateful is to recognize the love of God in everything He has given us— and He has given us everything. Every breath we draw is a gift of His love, every moment of existence a gift of grace.

THOMAS MERTON

November 25

All of you, live in harmony with one another; be sympathetic, love as brothers, be compassionate and humble. Do not repay evil with evil or insult with insult, but with blessing, because to this you were called so that you may inherit a blessing.

1 PETER 3:8-9

February 7

On Thanksgiving Day, I'll say a
little prayer,
To thank our heavenly Father for
things so rare:
For our parents, kind and dear,
For our friends both far and near....
All these things I'm thankful for,
Yes, all of these and many more.

KRISTY WOODWARD, AGE 11

November 24

The very possibility of friendship
with God transfigures life. This
conviction...tends inevitably to deepen
every human friendship, to make
it vastly more significant.

HENRY CHURCHILL KING

February **8**

Friendship is born at that moment when one person says to another: "What! You, too? Thought I was the only one."

C. S. LEWIS

November 23

I have learned that to have a good friend
is the purest of all God's gifts, for it is a love
that has no exchange of payment.

FRANCES FARMER

February **9**

Sing to the Lord a new song,
His praise in the assembly of the saints.
Let Israel rejoice in their Maker;
let the people of Zion be glad in
their King.
Let them praise His name with dancing
and make music to Him with
tambourine and harp.
For the Lord takes delight in His people;
He crowns the humble with salvation.

PSALM 149:1-4

November 22

There can be no intimacy
without conversation. To know
and love a friend over the years
you must have regular talks.

ALLAN LOY MCGINNIS

February 10

A slender acquaintance with the world must convince every man that actions, not words, are the true criterion of the attachment of friends.

GEORGE WASHINGTON

November **21**

We wait in hope for the Lord;
He is our help and our shield.
In Him our hearts rejoice,
for we trust in His holy name.
May Your unfailing love rest upon us, O Lord,
even as we put our hope in You.

PSALM 33:20-22

February 11

True friendships are lasting because
true love is eternal. A friendship in
which heart speaks to heart is a gift
from God, and no gift that comes
from God is temporary or occasional.
All that comes from God participates
in God's eternal life.

HENRI NOUWEN

November **20**

Friendship with God is a two-way street....
Jesus said that He tells
His friends all that His Father
has told Him; close friends
communicate thoroughly and make
a transfer of heart and thought.
How awesome is our opportunity
to be friends with God,
the almighty Creator of all!

February 12

Every day under the sun is a gift. Receive it with eagerness. Treat it kindly. Share it with joy. Each night return it to the Giver who will make it bright and shiny again before the next sunrise.

November 19

Having someone who understands
is a great blessing for ourselves.
Being someone who understands
is a great blessing to others.

JANETTE OKE

February 13

Sing to the Lord with thanksgiving;
make music to our God on the harp.
He covers the sky with clouds;
He supplies the earth with rain…
and makes grass grow on the hills….
He provides food for the cattle
and for the young ravens when they call.

PSALM 147:7-9

November **18**

A blessed thing it is for any man
or woman to have a friend, one human
soul whom we can trust utterly,
who knows the best and worst of us,
and who loves us in spite of all our faults.

CHARLES KINGSLEY

February **14**

The warmth of a friend's presence brings joy to our hearts, sunlight to our souls, and pleasure to all of life.

November **17**

Carry each other's burdens, and in this way you will fulfill the law of Christ.

GALATIANS 6:2

February **15**

Thanksgiving is a time of quiet reflection
upon the past and an annual reminder
that God has, again, been ever so faithful.
The solid and simple things of life are
brought into clear focus.

CHARLES SWINDOLL

November **16**

When I recollect the treasure of friendship
that has been bestowed upon me, I
withdraw all charges against life.
If much has been denied me, much, very
much has been given me. So long as the
memory of certain beloved friends lives
in my heart, I shall say that life is good.

HELEN KELLER

February 16

There's happiness in little things,
There's joy in passing pleasure;
But friendships are, from year to year,
The best of all life's treasure.

November **15**

We human beings can survive the most difficult of circumstances if we are not forced to stand against them alone.

JAMES DOBSON

February **17**

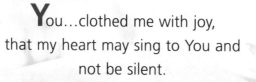

You...clothed me with joy,
that my heart may sing to You and
not be silent.
O Lord my God, I will give You
thanks forever.

PSALM 30:11-12

November 14

I breathed a song into the air;
It fell to earth, I know not where....
and the song, from beginning to end,
I found again in the heart of a friend.

LONGFELLOW

February **18**

You don't just luck into things
as much as you would like to think
you do. You build step by step, whether
it is friendships or opportunities.

BARBARA BUSH

November **13**

If I speak in the tongues of men and of angels, but have not love, I am only a resounding gong or a clanging cymbal.

1 CORINTHIANS 13:1

February 19

The mind is so rarely disturbed,
but that the company of a friend
will restore it to some degree
of tranquillity and sedateness.

ADAM SMITH

November 12

Knowing what to say is not always necessary; just the presence of a caring friend can make a world of difference.

SHERI CURRY

February **20**

It's good to have money and the things that money can buy, but it's good, too, to check up once in a while and make sure you haven't lost the things that money can't buy.

GEORGE HORACE LORIMER

November 11

I count your friendship one of the
chiefest pleasures of my life, a comfort
in time of doubt and trouble, a joy
in time of prosperity and success,
and an inspiration at all times.

EDWIN OSGOOD GROVER

February **21**

Do not forsake your friend and the friend of your father, and do not go to your brother's house when disaster strikes you—better a neighbor nearby than a brother far away.

PROVERBS 27:10

November **10**

True friendship speaks with gentle hands
To strengthen one in need,
With loving care and deep concern
As its most special creeds.

CRAIG E. SATHOFF

February **22**

Because we are His children,
God hears our [requests]. The King of
creation gives special heed to the voice of
His family. He is not only willing to hear us,
He loves to hear us.

MAX LUCADO

November 9

Be completely humble and gentle; be
patient, bearing with one another in love.
Make every effort to keep the unity of the
Spirit through the bond of peace.

EPHESIANS 4:2-3

February 23

Some blessings—like rainbows after rain or a friend's listening ear—are extraordinary gifts waiting to be discovered in an ordinary day.

November **8**

We are most of us very lonely in this world; you who have any who love you, cling to them and thank God.

WILLIAM MAKEPEACE THACKERAY

February **24**

A friend is somebody who loves us with understanding, as well as emotion.

ROBERT LOUIS STEVENSON

November 7

How many, many friendships
Life's path has let me see;
I've kept a scrap of each of them
To make the whole of me.

JUNE MASTERS BACHER

February **25**

Let us then approach the throne
of grace with confidence, so that
we may receive mercy and find grace
to help us in our time of need.

HEBREWS 4:16

November **6**

It is a good and safe rule to sojourn in every place as if you meant to spend your life there, never omitting an opportunity of doing a kindness, or speaking a true word, or making a friend.

JOHN RUSKIN

February **26**

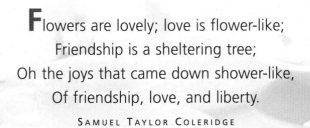

Flowers are lovely; love is flower-like;
Friendship is a sheltering tree;
Oh the joys that came down shower-like,
Of friendship, love, and liberty.

SAMUEL TAYLOR COLERIDGE

November 5

Finally, brothers, whatever is true, whatever is noble, whatever is right, whatever is pure, whatever is lovely, whatever is admirable—if anything is excellent or praiseworthy—think about such things. Whatever you have learned or received or heard from me, or seen in me—put it into practice. And the God of peace will be with you.

PHILIPPIANS 4:8-9

February 27

Lord Jesus Christ, I thank You
For all the benefits You have won for me,
For all the pains and insults that You have
borne for me....
May I know You more clearly,
Love You more dearly
And follow You more nearly
Day by day.
Amen.

RICHARD OF CHINCHESTER

November 4

I'd like to be the sort of friend that you
have been to me,
I'd like to be the help that you've been
always glad to be;
I'd like to mean as much to you each
minute of the day
As you have meant, old friend of mine, to
me along the way.

EDGAR A. GUEST

February **28**

If we understand our first and sole
duty to consist of loving God
supremely and loving everyone,
even our enemies, for God's dear sake,
then we can enjoy spiritual tranquility under
every circumstance.

A. W. TOZER

November 3

Character is like a tree and reputation like its shadow. The shadow is what we think of it; the tree is the real thing.

ABRAHAM LINCOLN

February 29

Give thanks to the Lord, for He is good.
His love endures forever....
to Him who alone does great wonders,
His love endures forever....
Give thanks to the God of heaven.
His love endures forever.

PSALM 136:1, 4, 26

November **2**

Let a person set their heart only
on doing the will of God
and they are instantly free.

A.W. TOZER

March 1

Joy is prayer—Joy is strength—Joy is love…she gives most who gives with joy. The best way to show our gratitude to God…is to accept everything with joy. A joyful heart is the inevitable result of a heart burning with love.

MOTHER TERESA

November 1

Dear friends, let us love one another, for love comes from God. Everyone who loves has been born of God and knows God.

1 John 4:7

March 2

A friend is a precious possession
Whose value increases with the years.
Someone who doesn't forsake us
when a difficult moment appears.

HENRY VAN DYKE

October **31**

We cannot rebuild the world by ourselves,
but we can have a small
part in it by beginning where we are.
It may only be taking care of a
neighbor's child or inviting someone
to dinner, but it is important.

DONNA L. GLAZIER

March 3

It is not what you give your friend,
but what you are willing to give her that
determines the quality of friendship.

MARY DIXON THAYER

October **30**

Great works do not always lie in our way,
but every moment we may do little ones
excellently, that is, with great love.

FRANCIS DE SALES

March **4**

The Lord gives strength to His people;
the Lord blesses His people with peace.

PSALM 29:11

October **29**

Love has hands to help others.
It has feet to hasten to the poor
and needy.
It has eyes to see misery and want.
It has ears to hear the sighs and
sorrows of men.
This is what love looks like.

AUGUSTINE

March 5

Celebrate the happiness
that friends are always giving;
make every day a holiday
and celebrate just living!

AMANDA BRADLEY

October **28**

Do not be afraid, little flock, for your
Father has been pleased to give you the
kingdom. Sell your possessions and give
to the poor. Provide purses for yourselves
that will not wear out, a treasure in
heaven that will not be exhausted,
where no thief comes near and no moth
destroys. For where your treasure is,
there your heart will be also.

LUKE 12:32-34

March 6

Friendship is the fruit gathered from
the trees planted in the rich soil of love,
and nurtured with tender
care and understanding.

ALMA L. WEIXELBAUM

October **27**

Whoever understands how to do a kindness when he fares well would be a friend better than any possession.

SOPHOCLES

March **7**

It is well that there is no one
without a fault; for she would not
have a friend in the world.

WILLIAM HAZLITT

October 26

Choices can change our lives profoundly.
The choice to mend a broken relationship,
to say "yes" to a difficult assignment,
to lay aside some important work to
play with a child, to visit some forgotten
person—these small choices may affect
many lives eternally.

GLORIA GAITHER

March **8**

I am like an olive tree
flourishing in the house of God.
I trust in God's unfailing love
for ever and ever.

PSALM 52:8

October 25

Gratitude unlocks the fullness of life.
It turns what we have into enough,
and more.... It can turn a meal into a
feast, a house into a home, a stranger
into a friend. It turns problems into
gifts, failures into successes,
the unexpected into perfect timing,
and mistakes into important events.

MELODY BEATTIE

March 9

Courage is what it takes to stand up and speak; courage is also what it takes to sit down and listen.

WINSTON CHURCHILL

October **24**

Each one should use whatever gift
he has received to serve others,
faithfully administering God's grace
in its various forms.

1 PETER 4:10

March 10

True friendship is a plant of slow growth, and must under-go and withstand the shocks of adversity before it is entitled to the appellation.

GEORGE WASHINGTON

October **23**

Generally, by the time you are Real, most of your hair has been loved off, and your eyes drop out and you get loose in the joints and very shabby. But these things don't matter at all, because once you are Real you can't be ugly, except to people who don't understand.

MARGERY WILLIAMS, *The Velveteen Rabbit*

March 11

I am speaking now of the highest duty we owe our friends, the noblest, the most sacred—that of keeping their own nobleness, goodness, pure and incorrupt.... If we let our friend become cold and selfish and exacting without a remonstrance, we are no true lover, no true friend.

HARRIET BEECHER STOWE

October 22

From quiet homes and first beginning
Out to the undiscovered ends,
There's nothing worth the wear of winning,
But laughter and the love of friends.

HILAIRE BELLOC

March **12**

I sought the Lord, and He answered me;
He delivered me from all my fears.

PSALM 34:4

October 21

Love is extravagant in the price it is willing to pay, the time it is willing to give, the hardships it is willing to endure, and the strength it is willing to spend.

JONI EARECKSON TADA

March 13

There is no friend like the old friend,
who has shared our morning days,
No greeting like their welcome,
no homage like their praise:
Fame is the scentless sunflower,
with gaudy crown of gold;
But friendship is the breathing rose,
with sweets in every fold.

OLIVER WENDELL HOLMES

October 20

Therefore, as God's chosen people, holy and dearly loved, clothe yourselves with compassion, kindness, humility, gentleness and patience.

COLOSSIANS 3:12

March **14**

I have learned that to have a good friend
is the purest of all God's gifts, for it is a love
that has no exchange of payment.

FRANCES FARMER

October **19**

Nothing opens the heart like a true
friend, to whom you may impart griefs,
joys, fears, hopes, and whatever
lies upon the heart.

FRANCIS BACON

March 15

The God who created the vast resources of the universe is also the inventor of the human mind. His inspired words of encouragement guarantee us that we can live above our circumstances.

JAMES DOBSON

October **18**

Friendship is precious, not only in the shade, but in the sunshine of life; and thanks to a benevolent arrangement of things, the greater part of life is sunshine.

THOMAS JEFFERSON

March **16**

This is how God showed His love among us: He sent His one and only Son into the world that we might live through Him.

1 JOHN 4:9

October **17**

May there always be work for your
hands to do;
May your purse always hold a coin or two;
May the sun always shine on
your windowpane;
May a rainbow be certain to follow
each rain;
May the hand of a friend always be near you;
May God fill your heart with gladness
to cheer you.

IRISH BLESSING

March **17**

Yes'm, old friends is always the best,
'less you can catch a new one that's
fit to make an old one out of.

SARAH ORNE JEWETT

October 16

Therefore, as God's chosen people, holy and dearly loved, clothe yourselves with compassion, kindness, humility, gentleness and patience. Bear with each other and forgive whatever grievances you may have against one another. Forgive as the Lord forgave you. And over all these virtues put on love, which binds them all together in perfect unity.

COLOSSIANS 3:12-14

March **18**

Called as partners in Christ's service,
Called to ministries of grace,
We respond with deep commitment
Fresh new lines of faith to trace.
May we learn the art of sharing,
Side by side and friend with friend,
Equal partners in our caring
To fulfill God's chosen end.

JANE PARKER HUBER

October 15

So long as we are loved by others
I should say that we are almost
indispensable; and no man is
useless while he has a friend.

ROBERT LOUIS STEVENSON

March 19

A true friendship is as wise as it is tender. The parties to it yield implicitly to the guidance of their love, and know no other law nor kindness.

HENRY DAVID THOREAU

October **14**

The best friendships have weathered
misunderstandings and trying times.
One of the secrets of a good relationship is
the ability to accept the storms.

ALAN LOY MCGINNIS

March 20

If you do away with the yoke
of oppression,
with the pointing finger and
malicious talk,
and if you spend yourselves in behalf
of the hungry
and satisfy the needs of the oppressed,
then your light will rise in the darkness,
and your night will become like
the noonday.

ISAIAH 58:9-10

October **13**

These things I warmly wish for you—
someone to love, some work to do,
a bit o' sun, a bit o' cheer,
and a Guardian Angel always near.

March 21

God's friendship is the unexpected
joy we find when we reach
His outstretched hand.

JANET L. WEAVER SMITH

October **12**

As the Father has loved Me, so have I loved you. Now remain in My love. If you obey My commands, you will remain in My love, just as I have obeyed My Father's commands and remain in His love. I have told you this so that My joy may be in you and that your joy may be complete.

JOHN 15:9-11

March **22**

Friendship cheers like a sunbeam;
charms like a good story; inspires like a
brave leader; binds like a golden chain;
guides like a heavenly vision.

NEWELL DWIGHT HILLIS

October **11**

Friends...they cherish each other's hopes.
They are kind to each other's dreams.

HENRY DAVID THOREAU

March 23

Talk is by far the most accessible of pleasures. It costs nothing in money, it is all profit, it completes our education, founds and fosters our friendships, and can be enjoyed at any age and in almost any state of health.

ROBERT LOUIS STEVENSON

October **10**

I wish you sunshine on your path and storms to season your journey.... I wish you faith—to help define your living and your life. More I cannot wish you except perhaps love to make all the rest worthwhile.

ROBERT A. WARD

March 24

You yourselves are our letter,
written on our hearts, known and read by
everybody. You show that you are a letter
from Christ, the result of our ministry,
written not with ink but with the Spirit
of the living God, not on tablets of stone
but on tablets of human hearts.

2 CORINTHIANS 3:2-3

October **9**

Friendship is nothing else than
an accord in all things, human and divine,
conjoined with mutual goodwill and
affection, and I am inclined to think that,
with the exception of wisdom, no better
thing has been given to man.

CICERO

March **25**

Don't walk in front of me,
I may not follow; Don't walk behind me,
I may not lead; Walk beside me,
and just be my friend.

ALBERT CAMUS

October **8**

The Lord is faithful to all His promises
and loving toward all He has made.
The Lord upholds all those who fall
and lifts up all who are bowed down.

PSALM 145:13-14

March 26

No man can look with undivided
vision at God and at the world
of reality so long as God and the world
are torn asunder.… But there is a place…
at which God and man have become
one.… It lies in the midst of history as a
divine miracle. It lies in Jesus Christ, the
reconciler of the world.

DIETRICH BONHOEFFER

October 7

God, who is love, simply cannot help but shed blessing upon blessing upon us. We do not need to beg, for He simply cannot help it!

HANNAH WHITALL SMITH

March **27**

May the Babe of Bethlehem be yours
to tend;
May the Boy of Nazareth be yours
for friend;
May the Man of Galilee His healing send;
May the Christ of Calvary His
courage lend;
May the Risen Lord His presence send;
And His holy angels defend you to the end.

"PILGRIM'S PRAYER"

October **6**

When we dream alone it remains only a dream. When we dream together, it is not just a dream; it is the beginning of reality.

DOM HELDER CAMARA

March **28**

May the Lord make your love increase and overflow for each other and for everyone else.

1 THESSALONIANS 3:12

October 5

The glory of friendship is found in the inspiration that comes when I discover that someone else believes in me and is willing to trust me with her friendship.

March **29**

The home you've always wanted,
the home you continue to long for
with all your heart, is the home
God is preparing for you!

ANNE GRAHAM LOTZ

October 4

We ought always to thank God for you,
brothers, and rightly so, because your faith
is growing more and more, and
the love every one of you has for
each other is increasing.

2 THESSALONIANS 1:3

March **30**

A friend is one who joyfully
sings with you when you are on
the mountain top, and silently walks
beside you through the valley.

WILLIAM A. WARD

October **3**

A rule I have had for years is:
to treat the Lord Jesus Christ
as a personal friend. His is not
a creed, a mere doctrine,
but it is He Himself we have.

DWIGHT L. MOODY

March **31**

Being a good friend, and having a good friend, can enrich your days and bring you lifelong satisfaction. But friendships don't just happen. They have to be created and nurtured. Like any other skill, building friendship has to be practiced.

SUE BROWDER

October **2**

Celebration is more than a happy
feeling. Celebration is an experience.
It is liking others, accepting others,
laughing with others.

DOUGLAS R. STUVA

April **1**

No one has ever seen God;
but if we love one another,
God lives in us and His love
is made complete in us.

1 JOHN 4:12

October 1

You will find, as you look back on your life, that...the moments when you have really lived, are the moments when you have done things in the spirit of love.

HENRY DRUMMOND

April **2**

Give to our God immortal praise;
Mercy and truth are all His ways;
He built the earth, He spread the sky,
And fixed the starry lights on high;
He sent His Son with power to save
From guilt and darkness and the grave;
Wonders of grace to God belong;
Repeat His mercies in your song.

ISAAC WATTS

September 30

Now that you have purified yourselves by obeying the truth so that you have sincere love for your brothers, love one another deeply, from the heart.

1 PETER 1:22

April **3**

Every man should keep a fair-sized
cemetery in which to bury the
faults of his friends.

HENRY WARD BEECHER

*Your sins have been forgiven
on account of His name.*

1 JOHN 2:12

September **29**

The best in me and the best in you
Hailed each other because they knew
That always and always since life began
Our being friends was part of God's plan.

GEORGE WEBSTER DOUGLAS

April 4

Gratitude. More aware of what you
have than what you don't. Recognizing the
treasure in the simple—a child's
hug, fertile soil, a golden sunset.
Relishing in the comfort of the common.

MAX LUCADO

September 28

[L]ord,] may I preach You with actions more than with words, with the example of my actions, with the visible light of the love that comes from You to my heart.

JOHN CARDINAL NEWMAN

April 5

Therefore each of you must put off falsehood and speak truthfully to his neighbor, for we are all members of one body. "In your anger do not sin": Do not let the sun go down while you are still angry, and do not give the devil a foothold.

EPHESIANS 4:25-27

September **27**

Open your hearts to the love God instills in them. God loves you tenderly. What He gives you is not to be kept under lock and key, but to be shared.

MOTHER TERESA

April 6

The best compliment to a child or a friend is the feeling you give her that she has been set free to make her own inquiries, to come to conclusions that are right for her, whether or not they coincide with your own.

ALISTAIR COOKE

September 26

Dear children, let us not love with words
or tongue but with actions and in truth.

1 JOHN 3:18

April 7

Joy is not the same as pleasure
or happiness.... Pleasure generally
comes from things, and always
through the senses; happiness comes
from humans through fellowship. Joy comes
from loving God and neighbor.

FULTON J. SHEEN

September 25

A true friend thinks of you when all others are thinking of themselves.

April 8

With an eye made quiet by the power
of harmony,
and the deep power of joy,
We see into the life of things.

WILLIAM WORDSWORTH

September **24**

Everyone was meant to share
God's all-abiding love and care;
He saw that we would need to know
a way to let these feelings show....
So God made hugs.

JILL WOLF

April **9**

Humble yourselves, therefore, under God's mighty hand, that He may lift you up in due time. Cast all your anxiety on Him because He cares for you.

1 PETER 5:6-7

September **23**

Do what you can to show you care about other people, and you will make our world a better place.

ROSALYNN CARTER

April 10

What sweetness is left in life
if you take away friendship? Robbing
life of friendship is like robbing
the world of the sun. A true friend is more
to be esteemed than kinsfolk.

CICERO

September **22**

Let us not become weary in doing good,
for at the proper time we will reap a harvest
if we do not give up. Therefore,
as we have opportunity, let us do good
to all people, especially to those who
belong to the family of believers.

GALATIANS 6:9-10

April 11

You have known your friend so long
and loved them so much, and then
all of a sudden you are so mad at
them, you say, I could just kill you and you
still like each other, because you
have always been friends and you
know in your mind you are going to
be friends in a few seconds anyway.

ANONYMOUS TWELVE-YEAR-OLD

September 21

Love is blind; friendship quietly
closes its eyes.

PAM BROWN

April 12

The man that hails you Tom or Jack,
And proves by thumps upon your back
How he esteems your merit,
Is such a friend, that one had need
Be very much his friend indeed
To pardon or to bear it.

WILLIAM COWPER

September 20

To know someone here or there
with whom you feel there is an
understanding in spite of distances
or thoughts unexpressed—that can
make of this earth a garden.

GOETHE

April **13**

May the God of hope fill you with all
joy and peace as you trust in Him.

ROMANS 15:13

September **19**

My fondest hope is that I may be worthy
of a place in your friendship,
and being admitted to that sacred
circle, that I may never prove
unfaithful to your trust in me.

EDWIN OSGOOD GROVER

April **14**

Friendship is one of the sweetest
joys of life. Many might have failed
beneath the bitterness of their trial
had they not found a friend.

CHARLES HADDON SPURGEON

September **18**

Let us hold unswervingly to the hope we profess, for He who promised is faithful. And let us consider how we may spur one another on toward love and good deeds.

HEBREWS 10:23-24

April **15**

Friends are of utmost importance. We love, trust, get hurt, sometimes get mad, but we love and trust anyhow, because that's the best way to let our friendship grow.

September **17**

Friendship: It involves many things but, above all, the power of going out of one's self and seeing and appreciating whatever is noble and loving in another.

THOMAS HUGHES

April **16**

To act the part of a true friend requires
more conscientious feeling than to fill
with credit and complacency any other
station or capacity in social life.

SARAH ELLIS

September **16**

Through the eyes of our friends, we learn to see ourselves...through the love of our friends, we learn to love ourselves... through the caring of our friends, we learn what it means to be ourselves completely.

April **17**

Dear friends, since God so loved us,
we also ought to love one another.

1 JOHN 4:11

September **15**

Human love and the delights
of friendship, out of which are built
the memories that endure, are also
to be treasured up as hints
of what shall be hereafter.

BEDE JARRETT

April **18**

For there is no friend like [you]
In calm or stormy weather;
To cheer one on the tedious way,
To fetch one if one goes astray,
To lift one if one totters down,
To strengthen whilst one stands.

CHRISTINA ROSSETTI

September 14

Every good and perfect gift is from above,
coming down from the Father
of the heavenly lights, who does not
change like shifting shadows.

JAMES 1:17

April **19**

If we would build on a sure foundation
in friendship, we must love friends
for their sake rather than for our own.

CHARLOTTE BRONTË

September **13**

Friends that hold each other accountable usually have a deep, abiding, and open relationship.... Being aware that a friend cares enough to make us accountable creates a stronger bond.

April **20**

A friend is someone who knows the song in your heart and sings it back to you when you have forgotten how it goes.

September **12**

Our loving God has provided a way
for us to be not only in fellowship
with Him, but also in fellowship with other
people.... We all need friends.

LANNY MCFARLAND

April 21

Get rid of all bitterness, rage and
anger, brawling and slander, along
with every form of malice. Be kind and
compassionate to one another,
forgiving each other, just as in Christ
God forgave you.

Ephesians 4:31-32

September 11

My friend is not perfect—no more than I am—and so we suit each other admirably.

ALEXANDER SMITH

April **22**

A woman is like a tea bag—
you never know how strong she
is until she gets in hot water.

ELEANOR ROOSEVELT

September 10

Live in peace with each other.
And we urge you, brothers, warn those
who are idle, encourage the timid, help the
weak, be patient with everyone.
Make sure that nobody pays back wrong for
wrong, but always try to be kind
to each other and to everyone else.

1 THESSALONIANS 5:13-14

April 23

We must love our friend so much that she shall be associated with our purest and holiest thoughts alone.

HENRY DAVID THOREAU

September **9**

Friendship is based upon
What we give, not what we take,
And it steers its kindly course
For a special friend's own sake.

EDITH H. SHANK

April 24

The things I want to know are in books;
my best friend is the person who'll
get me a book I ain't read.

ABRAHAM LINCOLN

September **8**

Laughing at ourselves as well
as with each other gives a surprising
sense of togetherness.

HAZEL C. LEE

April 25

Many are the woes of the wicked,
but the Lord's unfailing love
surrounds the man who trusts in Him.

PSALM 32:10

September 7

Bless God for the love of friends so true,
A love akin to His,
Which knows our faults and loves us still;
That's what real friendship is.

PAT LASSEN

April 26

Praise to Christ who feeds the hungry,
frees the captive, finds the lost,
Heals the sick, upsets religion, fearless
both of fate and cost.
Celebrate Christ's constant presence—
Friend and Stranger, Guest and Host.

IONA COMMUNITY HYMN

September 6

Bear with each other and forgive whatever grievances you may have against one another. Forgive as the Lord forgave you.

COLOSSIANS 3:13

April **27**

God's care is more evident in some instances than in others; and upon such instances people seize, and call them providences. It is well that they can; but it would be gloriously better if they could believe that the whole matter is one grand providence.

GEORGE MACDONALD

September **5**

True Blue Friends...make you feel good and warm; they are automatically on the same wavelength; they feel genuinely sorry and come to your assistance when you're in trouble...they really listen; they care about what you're doing.

ADELAIDE BRY

April **28**

It is an awesome, challenging thought: The Lord comes to us in our friends. What we do and are to them is an expression of what we are to Him.

LLOYD JOHN OGILVIE

September 4

If you want to be happy for a year,
plant a garden;
If you want to be happy for life,
plant a tree.

ENGLISH PROVERB

April 29

This is the message you heard
from the beginning: We should
love one another.

1 JOHN 3:11

September 3

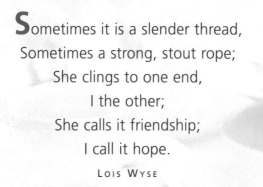

Sometimes it is a slender thread,
Sometimes a strong, stout rope;
She clings to one end,
I the other;
She calls it friendship;
I call it hope.

LOIS WYSE

April **30**

A really tight friendship is when you
start to really care about the person.
If they get sick, you kind of start worrying
about them—or if they get hit by a car.
An everyday friend, you say, I know
that kid, he or she's all right, and you
don't really think much of them.
But a close friend you worry about
more than yourself. Well, maybe
not more, but about the same.

ANONYMOUS FIFTEEN-YEAR-OLD

September 2

[Love] always protects, always trusts,
always hopes, always perseveres.

1 CORINTHIANS 13:7

May 1

All sicknesses have cures. The only
one that cannot be cured
is the sickness of feeling unloved.

MOTHER TERESA

For we know, brothers loved by God,
that He has chosen you.

1 THESSALONIANS 1:4

September 1

The capacity for caring illuminates any relationship. The more people you care about, and the more intensely you care, the more alive you are.

May **2**

Hope is definitely not the same thing as optimism. It is not the conviction that something will turn out well, but the certainty that something makes sense, regardless of how it turns out.

VÁCLAV HAVEL

August **31**

Friends run across the road with a plate of
freshly baked scones.
Friends fetch you to see the newly
born kittens....
Friends clear off your side of
the driveway.
Friends stop the papers when
you forgot....
Friends are absolutely indispensable.

JUDITH C. GRANT

May **3**

Never lose sight of the fact that the most important yardstick of your success will be how you treat other people—your family, friends, and coworkers, and even strangers you meet along the way.

BARBARA BUSH

August **30**

My friend. You never expect too much of me. You are glad when I succeed, but failure makes no difference to you. You give me all the help you can—but, more important, you are simply there.

WENDY JEAN SMITH

May 4

[L]ove] is not rude, it is not self-seeking,
it is not easily angered,
it keeps no record of wrongs.

1 CORINTHIANS 13:5

August **29**

In view of God's mercy…offer your
bodies as living sacrifices, holy and pleasing
to God—this is your
spiritual act of worship. Do not
conform any longer to the pattern
of this world, but be transformed
by the renewing of your mind.

ROMANS 12:1-2

May 5

When we honestly ask ourselves which
person in our lives means the most to us,
we often find that it is those who, instead
of giving much advice, solutions, or cures,
have chosen rather to…be silent with us
in a moment of despair or confusion…
[to] stay with us in an hour of grief and
bereavement…. That is a friend who cares.

HENRI NOUWEN

August **28**

One thing life has taught me: if you are interested, you never have to look for new interests. They come to you. When you are genuinely interested in one thing, it will always lead to something else.

ELEANOR ROOSEVELT

May **6**

Oh, a friend! How true is that old saying,
that the enjoyment of one is sweeter and
more necessary than that
of the elements of water and fire!

MICHEL DE MONTAIGNE

August **27**

A friend is a close companion
on rainy days,
someone to share with through
every phase...
Forgiving and helping to bring
out the best,
believing the good and forgetting
the rest.

May **7**

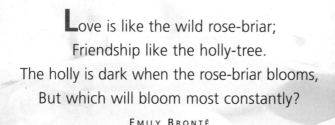

Love is like the wild rose-briar;
Friendship like the holly-tree.
The holly is dark when the rose-briar blooms,
But which will bloom most constantly?

EMILY BRONTË

August 26

For memory has painted this perfect day,
with colors that never fade.
And we find at the end of a perfect day,
the soul of a friend we've made.

CARRIE JACOBS BOND

May 8

The crucible for silver and the furnace
for gold,
but man is tested by the praise
he receives.

PROVERBS 27:21

August 25

Let love and faithfulness never leave you;
bind them around your neck,
write them on the tablet of your heart.
Then you will win favor and a good name
in the sight of God and man.

PROVERBS 3:3-4

May 9

Reflect on your present blessings,
of which every man has many;
not on your past misfortunes,
of which all men have some.

CHARLES DICKENS

August **24**

True friendship can afford true knowledge.
It does not depend on darkness and
ignorance. A want of discernment cannot
be an ingredient in it.

HENRY DAVID THOREAU

May **10**

The love of our neighbor in all its
fullness simply means being able to say,
"What are you going through?"

SIMONE WEIL

August 23

The best and most beautiful things in the
world cannot be seen or even touched.
They must be felt with the heart.

HELEN KELLER

May 11

Character is so largely affected by associations that we cannot afford to be indifferent as to who and what our friends are. They write their names in our albums, but they do more, they help make us what we are. Be therefore careful in selecting them; and when wisely selected, never sacrifice them.

M. HULBURD

August 22

Without friends the world is but a wilderness. There is no one that imparts her joy to her friends, but she receives more joy; and no one that imparts her grievances to her friends, but she grieves the less.

FRANCIS BACON

May 12

A man of many companions may
come to ruin,
but there is a friend who sticks closer
than a brother.

PROVERBS 18:24

August **21**

And I pray that you, being rooted and established in love, may have power, together with all the saints, to grasp how wide and long and high and deep is the love of Christ, and to know this love that surpasses knowledge—that you may be filled to the measure of all the fullness of God.

EPHESIANS 3:17-19

May 13

Friends are those rare people
who ask how we are and then
wait to hear the answer.

ED CUNNINGHAM

August 20

To smile at someone who is sad;
to visit, even for a little while, someone
who is lonely; to give someone shelter
from the rain with our umbrella;
to read something for someone who is
blind: these and others can be small
things, very small things, but they are
appropriate to give our love of God
concrete expression to the poor.

MOTHER TERESA

May 14

Stand outside this evening. Look at the stars. Know that you are special and loved by the One who created them.

August **19**

The fountain of beauty is the heart, and every generous thought illustrates the walls of your chamber.

FRANCIS QUARLES

May 15

Choose your friend wisely,
Test your friend well;
True friends, like rarest gems,
Prove hard to tell,
Winter him, summer him.
Know your friend well.

August **18**

Some people are so special that once they
enter your life, it becomes richer
and fuller and more wonderful than
you ever thought it could be.

May **16**

Humble yourselves, therefore, under God's mighty hand, that He may lift you up in due time.

1 PETER 5:6

August **17**

Be kind and compassionate
to one another, forgiving each other,
just as in Christ God forgave you.

EPHESIANS 4:32

May 17

I cannot count the number of times
I have been strengthened by another
woman's heartfelt hug, appreciative
note, surprise gift, or caring questions...
my friends are an oasis
to me, encouraging me to go on.
They are essential to my well-being.

DEE BRESTIN

August **16**

Favorite people, favorite places,
favorite memories of the past...
These are the joys of a lifetime...
these are the things that last.

May **18**

If you can help anybody even a little,
be glad; up the steps of usefulness
and kindness, God will lead you
on to happiness and friendship.

MALTBIE D. BABCOCK

August 15

Blessed are they who have
the gift of making friends,
for it is one of God's best gifts.

THOMAS HUGHES

May **19**

Somehow, when the going gets rough and our protective covering is stripped away, close, tender moments come about more freely, and lasting friendships are formed.

JERE KESSLER CORVEN

August **14**

Next to knowing when to seize
an opportunity, the most important
thing in life is to know when
to forgo an advantage.

BENJAMIN DISRAELI

May **20**

Praise the Lord with the harp;
make music to Him on the ten-stringed lyre.
Sing to Him a new song;
play skillfully, and shout for joy.
For the word of the Lord is right and true,
He is faithful in all He does.

PSALM 33:2-4

August 13

He who dwells in the shelter
of the Most High
will rest in the shadow of the Almighty.

PSALM 91:1

May **21**

In time we can accept a great loss
if we have somebody loving us through it.
God sends friends and companions
to love and support us.

ROBERT SCHULLER

August 12

I am still determined to be cheerful and happy, in whatever situation I may be; for I have also learned from experience that the greater part of our happiness or misery depends upon our dispositions, and not upon our circumstances.

MARTHA WASHINGTON

May 22

Jesus' love does not depend upon
what we do for Him. Not at all.
In the eyes of the King, you have
value simply because you are.

MAX LUCADO

August 11

All truly wise thoughts have been thought already thousands of times; but to make them truly ours, we must think them over again honestly, till they take root in our personal experience.

GOETHE

May **23**

God's forgiveness and love exist for you
as if you were the only person on earth.

CECIL OSBORNE

August 10

Friends warm you with their presence, trust you with their secrets, and remember you in their prayers.

May **24**

Live in harmony with one another.
Do not be proud, but be willing to
associate with people of low position.
Do not be conceited.

ROMANS 12:16

August **9**

Love is patient, love is kind. It does not envy, it does not boast, it is not proud.

1 CORINTHIANS 13:4

May 25

Do not use a hatchet to remove
a fly from your friend's forehead.

CHINESE PROVERB

August 8

Friends...lift our spirits, keep us honest,
stick with us when times are tough,
and make mundane tasks enjoyable.
No wonder we want to make friends.

EMILY GRIFFIN

May **26**

Whatever one possesses becomes of double value when we have the opportunity of sharing it with others.

JEAN-NICOLAS BOUILLY

August **7**

Give God the praise for
any well-spent day.

SUSANNA WESLEY

May **27**

When it's hard to look back, and you're scared to look ahead, you can look beside you and your best friend will be there.

August **6**

A friend listens with her eyes and her heart...and understands what you can't put into words.

May **28**

The Lord is good to those whose
hope is in Him,
to the one who seeks Him.

LAMENTATIONS 3:25

August 5

Love must be sincere. Hate what is evil; cling to what is good. Be devoted to one another in brotherly love. Honor one another above yourselves.

ROMANS 12:9-10

May 29

A knowledge that another has felt
as we have felt, and seen things
not much otherwise than we have seen
them, will continue to the end to
be one of life's choicest blessings.

ROBERT LOUIS STEVENSON

August **4**

Friendship! mysterious cement
of the soul!
Sweetener of life! and solder of society!

ROBERT BLAIR

May **30**

If faith is scarce, it is because there
is too much selfishness in the world,
too much egoism. Faith, in order to be
authentic, has to be generous and giving.
Love and faith go hand in hand.

MOTHER TERESA

August 3

Friends stay in contact, they talk about things that matter to both of them, they're honest, they're supportive, they're willing to give something.

PHIL MCGRAW

May 31

Give Your light through me, [Lord],
and remain in me in such a way that
every soul I come in contact with
can feel Your presence in me.

JOHN CARDINAL NEWMAN

August 2

Fame is the scentless sunflower,
with gaudy crown of gold;
But friendship is the breathing rose,
with sweets in every fold.

OLIVER WENDELL HOLMES

June **1**

You are the light of the world. A city on a hill cannot be hidden. Neither do people light a lamp and put it under a bowl. Instead they put it on its stand, and it gives light to everyone in the house. In the same way, let your light shine before men, that they may see your good deeds and praise your Father in heaven.

MATTHEW 5:14-16

August 1

O Lord, You have searched me
and You know me.
You know when I sit and when I rise;
You perceive my thoughts from afar.
You discern my going out and my
lying down;
You are familiar with all my ways.
Before a word is on my tongue
You know it completely, O Lord.

PSALM 139:1-4

June 2

We walk without fear, full of hope
and courage and strength to do His will,
waiting for the endless good which
He is always giving as fast as
He can get us able to take it in.

GEORGE MACDONALD

July **31**

In the give and take of genuine relationship, as "iron sharpens iron," the imprint of the true friend becomes indelible on the soul of the other.

MICHAEL CARD

June 3

Moments spent listening, talking, playing,
and sharing together may be
the most important times of all.

GLORIA GAITHER

July **30**

The dearest friends are the
auldest friends,
And the young are just on trial.

ROBERT LOUIS STEVENSON

June **4**

In poverty and other misfortunes
of life, true friends are a sure refuge.
The young they keep out of mischief; to
the old they are a comfort and aid in their
weakness, and those in the prime
of life they incite to noble deeds.

ARISTOTLE

July 29

Friends are angels who lend us their wings when our wings have forgotten how to fly.

June 5

Therefore confess your sins to each other and pray for each other so that you may be healed. The prayer of a righteous man is powerful and effective.

JAMES 5:16

July 28

My purpose is that they may be
encouraged in heart and united in love,
so that they may have the full riches of
complete understanding, in order that
they may know the mystery of God,
namely, Christ, in whom are hidden all
the treasures of wisdom and knowledge.

COLOSSIANS 2:2-3

June **6**

There is nourishment from being encouraged and held up by others when we are weak. We are nourished from feedback from friends whom we trust and who will be honest with us.

RICH G. BUHLER

July **27**

Thank you, Lord, for the grace of Your love,
for the grace of friendship,
and for the grace of beauty.

HENRI NOUWEN

June 7

If a person does not make new acquaintances as she advances through life, she will soon find herself left alone. A person…should keep her friendship in a constant repair.

SAMUEL JOHNSON

July 26

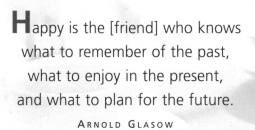

Happy is the [friend] who knows
what to remember of the past,
what to enjoy in the present,
and what to plan for the future.

ARNOLD GLASOW

June **8**

Just don't give up trying to do
what you really want to do.
Where there is love and inspiration,
I don't think you can go wrong.

ELLA FITZGERALD

July 25

Friends are an indispensable part
of a meaningful life. They are the
ones who share our burdens
and multiply our blessings.

BEVERLY LAHAYE

June **9**

Two are better than one,
because they have a good return
for their work:
If one falls down,
his friend can help him up.
But pity the man who falls
and has no one to help him up!

ECCLESIASTES 4:9-10

July 24

I thank my God every time I remember you.
In all my prayers for all of you,
I always pray with joy because
of your partnership in the gospel
from the first day until now.

PHILIPPIANS 1:3-5

June 10

There's all of pleasure and all of peace
In a friend or two;
And all your troubles may find release...
With a friend or two.

WILBUR D. NESBIT

July 23

We must know that we have been
created for greater things, not just
to be a number in the world, not
just to go for diplomas and degrees,
this work and that work. We have been
created in order to love and to be loved.

MOTHER TERESA

June 11

We have not made ourselves; we are
the gift of the living God to one another.

REINE DUELL BETHANY

July 22

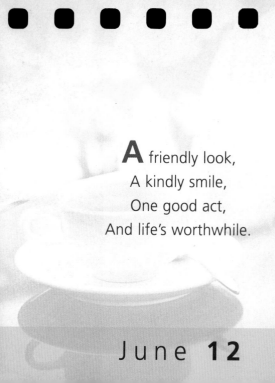

A friendly look,
A kindly smile,
One good act,
And life's worthwhile.

June **12**

Do all the good you can, by all the
means you can, in all the ways you can,
in all the places you can, at all the times
you can, to all the people you can,
as long as ever you can.

JOHN WESLEY

July **21**

If you lose money you lose much,
If you lose friends you lose more,
If you lose faith you lose all.

ELEANOR ROOSEVELT

June **13**

Blessed are the merciful,
for they will be shown mercy.
Blessed are the pure in heart,
for they will see God.
Blessed are the peacemakers,
for they will be called sons of God.

MATTHEW 5:7-9

July **20**

My command is this: Love each other
as I have loved you. Greater love has
no one than this, that he lay down
his life for his friends. You are
My friends if you do what I command.

JOHN 15:12-14

June **14**

Encouragement is awesome.
It has the capacity to…actually
change the course of another
human being's day, week, or life.

CHARLES SWINDOLL

July **19**

When you're with someone you trust in,
never needing to pretend,
Someone who helps you know yourself...
you know you're with a friend.

AMANDA BRADLEY

June 15

A good friend is a connection to life—
a tie to the past, a road to the future, the
key to sanity in a totally insane world.

LOIS WYSE

July **18**

When we treat a person as they are,
we make them worse than they are;
when we treat them as if they already were
what they potentially could be,
we make them what they should be.

GOETHE

June **16**

God makes our lives a medley
of joy and tears, hope and help,
love and encouragement.

July **17**

Friends remind us we are part of
something greater than ourselves,
a larger world, and the right
friends keep us on track.

BARBARA JENKINS

June 17

Even though I walk
through the valley of the shadow of death,
I will fear no evil,
for You are with me;
Your rod and Your staff,
they comfort me.

PSALM 23:4

July **16**

Do not let any unwholesome talk
come out of your mouths, but only
what is helpful for building others up
according to their needs, that it
may benefit those who listen.

EPHESIANS 4:29

June **18**

The true joy of life [is] being used for a purpose recognized by yourself as a mighty one.

GEORGE BERNARD SHAW

July **15**

But God has promised strength for the day,
Rest for the labor, light for the way,
Grace for the trials, help from above,
Unfailing sympathy, undying love.

ANNIE JOHNSON FLINT

June **19**

That is God's call to us—simply
to be people who are content to live
close to Him and to renew the kind
of life in which the closeness
is felt and experienced.

THOMAS MERTON

July **14**

A good friend will sharpen your character, draw your soul into the light, and challenge your heart to love in a greater way.

June **20**

The conversion from mistrust to trust
is a confident quest seeking the
spiritual meaning of human existence.
Grace abounds and walks around the edges
of our everyday experience.

BRENNAN MANNING

July **13**

Advice is like snow; the softer it falls, the longer it dwells upon, and the deeper it sinks into, the mind.

SAMUEL TAYLOR COLERIDGE

June 21

But if we walk in the light, as He is in the light, we have fellowship with one another, and the blood of Jesus, His Son, purifies us from all sin.

1 JOHN 1:7

July **12**

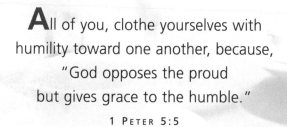

All of you, clothe yourselves with
humility toward one another, because,
"God opposes the proud
but gives grace to the humble."

1 PETER 5:5

June **22**

Who but a good friend would put her life on hold in order to listen, advise, sympathize, and send you on your way secure in the knowledge that someone cares?

LOIS WYSE

July **11**

May God's richest blessings
be upon you both today and
throughout the year—and may those
blessings flow through you to touch
the lives of everyone you meet.

GARY SMALLEY

June 23

A friend is a gift whose worth cannot be measured except by the heart.

CHARLES HANSON TOWNE

July **10**

A person should hear a little music, read a little poetry, and see a fine picture every day of his or her life, in order that worldly cares may not obliterate the sense of the beautiful which God has implanted in the human soul.

GOETHE

June **24**

We read more deeply, remember more clearly, enjoy events with greater pleasure if we have a friend to share with.

PAM BROWN

July **9**

Happiness is inward and not outward; and
so it does not depend on what we have,
but on what we are.

HENRY VAN DYKE

June 25

The Lord your God is with you,
He is mighty to save.
He will take great delight in you,
He will quiet you with His love,
He will rejoice over you with singing.

ZEPHANIAH 3:17

July 8

Blessed are the ones God sends
to show His love for us—our friends.

June **26**

Let God have you, and let God love you—and don't be surprised if your heart begins to hear music you've never heard and your feet learn to dance as never before.

MAX LUCADO

July **7**

The world is moving so fast these days that the one who says it can't be done is generally interrupted by someone doing it.

HARRY EMERSON FOSDICK

June **27**

The depth of a friendship—how much it means to us...depends, at least in part, upon how many parts of ourselves a friend sees, shares, and validates.

LILLIAN RUBIN

July 6

There is something basic about friendship. It is like the structure that holds up a building. It is mostly hidden and absolutely essential.

EMILIE BARNES

June **28**

Let your conversation be always full of grace, seasoned with salt, so that you may know how to answer everyone.

COLOSSIANS 4:6

July 5

Common sense is the knack
of seeing things as they are, and doing
things as they ought to be done.

HARRIET BEECHER STOWE

June **29**

It is my ambition and desire to so administer the affairs of the government while I remain President that if at the end I have lost every other friend on earth I shall at least have one friend remaining and that one shall be down inside me.

ABRAHAM LINCOLN

July **4**

But the fruit of the Spirit is love, joy, peace, patience, kindness, goodness, faithfulness, gentleness and self-control.

GALATIANS 5:22-23

June **30**

The heart of a friend is a wondrous thing,
A gift of God most fair;
May I carefully tend the seed which grows
In friendship's garden there.

PAT LASSEN

July **3**

What made us friends in the long ago
When we first met?
Well, I think I know;
The best in me and the best in you
Hailed each other because they knew
That always and always since life began
Our being friends was part of God's plan.

GEORGE WEBSTER DOUGLAS

July **1**

No love, no friendship can cross
the path of our destiny without
leaving some mark on it forever.

FRANÇOIS MAURIAC

July **2**